ZOE:

The God-Kind of Life

Kenneth E. Hagin

Unless otherwise indicated, all Scripture quotations in this volume are from the *King James Version* of the Bible.

Seventh Printing 1997

ISBN 0-89276-402-3

In the U.S. write:
Kenneth Hagin Ministries
P.O. Box 50126
Tulsa, OK 74150-0126

In Canada write:
Kenneth Hagin Ministries
P.O. Box 335, Station D,
Etobicoke (Toronto), Ontario
Canada, M9A 4X3

Contents

Do not become discouraged
because the truth does not dawn
on your spirits all at once.
But keep meditating on the
facts of the Word.
The more you meditate on
that which is written,
And the more you meditate
on that which is said as one shall speak
under the anointing
and the inspiration of the Spirit,
then little by little it will become real to you.
And as on the inside of you,
in your spirit,
in your inner man,
it takes shape and form,
it will reshape your own spirit,
until you'll no longer be a
weakling, spiritually,
but you shall become strong,
and be able to stand,
and do the works the Lord
has called you unto,
and rule and reign and dominate in life,
as a king by Jesus Christ.
So do not turn away even because you do not
fully understand or see.
But let your mind be open and your spirit be
receptive and say thou,
"O blessed Holy Spirit,
unveil the truth unto my spirit,
that I may stand in the fullness

of the provision of my Father,
For He is my Father.
I love Him and He loves me."
And so you will become that which He has
ordained that you should become, and rise
up to the level of the full privileges,
and rights, and authority,
and dominion of a son of God.
Rejoice and be glad,
and speak forth the Word of Faith.
Speak unto those circumstances
that have you bound.
And command them to leave,
and so you shall be loosed.
Speak unto the storm that appears on the
horizon of you life,
and say,"Peace be still,"
and there will be calm.
Learn what is yours,
and act upon it.
And it shall become yours in reality.
Thank you, Lord Jesus!

— Prophecy given by
Kenneth E. Hagin
October 19, 1980,
RHEMA Bible Church,
Tulsa, Oklahoma

Chapter 1
What Is Zoe?

Why did Jesus come? To found a church? To improve on humanity or to give us a code of conduct? No, He came for one purpose: *". . . I am come that they might have life, and that they might have it more abundantly"* (John 10:10).

The Greek word translated "life" in this verse is *zoe.*

Zoe is the God-kind of life.

The Bible says, *"For God so loved the world, that he gave his only begotten Son, that whosoever believeth in him should not perish, but have everlasting life"* (John 3:16). And, *"For the wages of sin is death; but the gift of God is eternal life through Christ Jesus our Lord"* (Rom. 6:23).

This eternal life He came to give us is the nature of God. John 5:26 says, *"For as the Father hath life in himself; so hath he given to the Son to have life in himself."*

In John 1:4 we get the first intimation of what this life will do for us: *"In him was life; and the life was the light of men."* Light stands for development. In other words, "In Him was life; and the life was the *development* of men."

Or, "In Him was *zoe*; and the *zoe* was the development of men." John 5:26 could be translated, "For as the Father has *zoe* in Himself; so hath He given to the Son to have *zoe* in Himself."

1

There are four different Greek words translated "life" in the New Testament. First, there is *zoe*. Then there is *psuche*. That means natural or human life. *Bios* means manner of life. And *anastrophee* means confused behavior.

It seems strange that the church has majored on "manner of life" or "behavior" rather than eternal life, which determines in a very large way the manner of life.

No matter what manner of life or behavior you have, if you don't have eternal life, it won't amount to anything anyway.

Receiving eternal life is the most miraculous incident in life.

Often we call it conversion or the new birth. Some call it "getting religion," but that's not what it is, really.

It is, in reality, God imparting His very nature, substance, and being to our human spirits.

It is described by the Apostle Paul in Second Corinthians.

2 CORINTHIANS 5:17,18
17 Therefore if any man be in Christ, he is a new creature: old things are passed away; behold, all things are become new.
18 And all things are of God, who hath reconciled us to himself by Jesus Christ, and hath given to us the ministry of reconciliation.

This is the miraculous recreating of man. *"Therefore if any man be in Christ. . . ."* You understand Paul is not talking about the body, or the outward man, or the mind. He's talking about the spirit — the inward man — who is in Christ. God is actually giving birth to a new man.

In the new birth, our spirits are born of God. More than one of the prophets of the Old Testament prophesied that God would establish a New Covenant with the house of Israel. This covenant is the New Testament, as we know it. Concerning this new covenant, Ezekiel said:

> **EZEKIEL 36:26,27**
> **26 A new heart also will I give you, and a new spirit will I put within you: and I will take away the stony heart out of your flesh, and I will give you an heart of flesh.**
> **27 And I will put my spirit within you, and cause you to walk in my statutes, and ye shall keep my judgments, and do them.**

What he is prophesying about is the new birth. The words "heart" and "spirit" are used interchangeably. Your heart is your spirit.

When God is speaking of the heart of a man in His Word, He is speaking of the real you. A scripture that is illuminating on the subject is First Peter 3:4: *"But let it be the hidden man of the heart, in that which is not corruptible, even the ornament of a meek and quiet spirit, which is in the sight of God of great price."*

Peter, here, is talking to Christian wives, and he mentions the outward adorning of the flesh. He says, in effect, "Don't take all your time on your hair and clothes. But see to it that the inward man, or hidden man of the heart, is adorned first with a quiet and meek spirit.

Paul, in First Corinthians 9:27, says: *"But I keep under my body, and bring it into subjection: lest that by any means, when I have preached to others, I myself should be a castaway."*

Notice something. Paul said, *"I* keep under my body, and *I* bring it into subjection." What is he saying? He's saying, *"I* don't let my body rule me." You see, "I" is the man on the inside. If your body were you, Paul would have said, "I keep *myself* under." He calls the body "it." Who is "I"? "I" is the real you. That is, the inward man or hidden man of the heart.

With most people, their body rules their inward man. That is what makes carnal Christians.

1 CORINTHIANS 3:3
3   For ye are yet carnal: for whereas there is among you envying, and strife, and divisions, are ye not carnal, and walk as men?

Here Paul is telling the Corinthians they are carnal or baby Christians. One translation says "body ruled" instead of "carnal." He tells them they are living like people who have never been born again — like mere men.

Paul says something else interesting in writing to the Romans.

ROMANS 12:1,2
1   I beseech you therefore, brethren, by the mercies of God, that ye present your bodies a living sacrifice, holy, acceptable unto God, which is your reasonable service.

2 **And be not conformed to this world: but be ye**
transformed by the renewing of your mind, that ye
may prove what is that good, and acceptable, and
perfect, will of God.

Paul wasn't writing to the world. He was writing to
the saints at Rome. *"To all that be in Rome, beloved of*
God, called to be saints . . ." (Rom. 1:7). He said *you* do
something with your body. If *you* don't do anything with
it, nothing will ever be done.

Second Corinthians 5:17 says, *"Therefore if any*
man. . . ." What is Paul talking about? Does he mean
the outward man? No, it couldn't be the outward man,
because he said, *". . . if any man be in Christ, he is a*
new creature. . . ."

It is the life and nature of God coming into your
spirit that makes you a new creature. It makes the
inward man a new man.

The body is not new. Thank God, at the coming of
the Lord, we will have a new body. This new man, the
hidden man of the heart, is to dominate the body. The
body is not to dominate you.

Paul not only talks about doing something with the
body, but in Romans 12:2 he talks about renewing the
mind. He is writing to people who are born again and
Spirit filled, yet they need to do something with their
bodies and minds.

One of the greatest needs of church members today
is to have renewed minds. Your mind becomes renewed
with the Word of God.

We know this then: Man is a spirit. We know he is in the same class with God, because God is a Spirit and because man was made to have fellowship with God. We've never majored on this fact as we ought. Therefore, we've never been able to walk in the light of eternal life as we ought.

Is the Spirit Perfect?

Some have wondered whether the reborn spirit, the new man in Christ, is perfect, or fully developed after receiving eternal life.

The spirit couldn't be perfect, because Peter says, *"As newborn babes, desire the sincere milk of the Word, that ye may grow thereby"* (1 Peter 2:2).

And Paul says, "I have not yet reached perfection . . ." (Phil. 3:12 *The New English Bible: New Testament).* Actually, the Greek word used there for perfection means *reaching maturity.*

Some people say, "I'm perfect and complete in Christ." Well, yes, you're a complete person, but you're not full grown. There are always people who are promiscuous about permitting sin and who want to excuse themselves by saying, "It was just my *body* that sinned; it wasn't my *spirit."*

But sin is a spiritual thing; it isn't just a physical thing. Paul said in writing to the Church at Corinth, *"Flee fornication. Every sin that a man doeth is without the body; but he that committeth fornication sinneth against his own body"* (1 Cor. 6:18). So if it's without the body, it has to be a spiritual thing. However, even fornication originates in your spirit. Your spirit has to give your body permission to sin or your body can't do it.

You are the custodian of your house. Remember Paul said, *"But I keep under my body, and bring it into subjection . . ."* (1 Cor. 9:27). You are responsible for what your body does. It all starts in your spirit. That's what Paul meant when he said, *". . . let us cleanse ourselves from all filthiness of the flesh and spirit . . ."* (2 Cor. 7:1). Don't let things that are wrong start in your spirit.

In Romans 6:6 it says, *"Knowing this, that our old man is crucified with him, that the body of sin might be destroyed, that henceforth we should not serve sin."* Some use that verse to say we are already redeemed — spirit, soul, and body. What does that verse mean?

The body of sin Paul is talking about is not the physical body; he's talking about the spirit man. You are a new creature. The old sin nature in your spirit is gone. The sin nature in your flesh is still there.

The problem is that the flesh nature still wants to do things that are wrong. It wants to keep on doing the things it always did. *If your mind is not renewed with the Word of God, it will side in with your flesh and dominate your spirit.* But if you get your *mind* renewed, your *spirit*, through your mind, will dominate your *body*.

The old man is the old spiritual man. You've still got the same body you had and the same mind you had. That old spiritual man had the nature of the devil in him. That is the nature that's gone, or the body of sin that's gone. It is up to us to put on the new man on the outside.

Many ask what the difference is between renewing
your mind and training your spirit. Actually, if you follow those principles involved in training the human
spirit (I have a tape series on the subject), your mind
will become renewed. What you are doing in renewing
your mind is training your mind to think in line with
God's Word. Even if the Word doesn't seem to be regis-
tering on your mind, it will speak to your spirit,
because it's spiritual food. By meditating upon it, your
mind becomes renewed.

You see, because your spirit becomes new when you
are born again, it will know things your head doesn't
know. Your spirit will try to tell you things the Word
already tells you but you just can't see them. That's
because your spirit picks up knowledge from the Spirit
of God.

Notice in James 1:21 it says, "*. . . receive with meek-
ness the engrafted word, which is able to save your
souls.*" That used to bother me before I separated spirit
and soul (Heb. 4:12), because I thought your soul was
saved if you were born again. You see, your spirit has
become a new man, but it is the Word of God which will
save your soul, or restore it.

Chapter 2

What Happens When You Receive Zoe?

Zoe, then, means eternal life, or God's life. This new kind of life is God's nature. It produces certain changes in man. You can see the effects of that life. Almost at once, you can see it in a person's habits. You can see it in his speech. It changes conduct, corrects habits, and forms new ones.

I remember the first church I pastored. I would walk out in the country, because I didn't have a car, stay Saturday night with a family, preach Sunday morning and Sunday night, and walk back into town Monday morning. I wore out four pairs of shoes the first year, walking to preach.

Once in a while I would catch a ride, but I would walk part of the way every time.

I stayed in the home of one particular family, and I thought this man was a Christian. I never did ask him, but I just assumed he was a Christian. He never missed church. He brought his family to every service.

He was a good man. He had family prayer at the table. He even read the Bible and prayed in the home, and he had no bad habits.

His two boys, both teenagers, said, "We've never heard our daddy and momma fuss." I thought he was saved. "And not only that," they said, "we've never heard our daddy use foul language or curse." He wouldn't even use slang. If he happened to be working and hit his finger, he wouldn't even say "shoot."

So I saw his life, his conduct; and we judge by conduct a lot of times.

I thought he must be saved, but I never took time to ask him. One Sunday night we were having an open-air revival, and when the evangelist gave the altar call, this man came to the altar. I couldn't believe my eyes. I had thought he was the best man in the church.

The next day the community was buzzing. People were saying, "That fellow went to the altar last night and he's the best man around. He lives a better life than anyone else. We thought he was already saved."

But he said to me, "My mother was old-time Holiness and she raised me that way. I always abided by her teaching, but I never had been saved. I had never been born again."

He had adjusted his conduct, but there hadn't been anything on the inside of him. People in town wondered if they would see any change in him.

They decided they did!

"In the first place," they said, "he looks different. There is a light on his face that never used to be there." (Notice the Bible says this life is the *light* of men.) Second, people heard a difference in his speech. He was kinder than ever. Even the sinners could see a difference. There was a new element that came into his spirit even though he had already been a good man.

People who have this eternal life are called "twice-born men." They are "new creation men." The life of God *will* have an effect on your life, habits, and qualities.

No criminals have this life, because if they have it, it will change them. We've got hundreds of people on our mailing list who are in prison, but they're not criminals anymore.

One young man wrote me from Ohio and said, "I'm still in prison, but I want you to know I'm the Lord's freed man. I'm free on the inside and I'm getting out of here. And when I get out, I'm going to preach."

I saw him at a Full Gospel Business Men's convention, and that's what he was doing — getting ready to preach.

We had a fellow who graduated from our school who had been in the Huntsville Penitentiary in Texas. he wrote me a letter and said he had gotten saved in prison. A Methodist minister would go in and have classes and give out my books there.

This young man said, "I got your big blue book on faith, and since I've become a new creature, I've been making my confession of faith. I told all the guards and my fellow prisoners that I was getting out (it was time for my parole).

"They said, 'You don't get out the first time you come up for parole when you killed a policeman.' (Under the influence of dope he had shot and killed a policeman.)

"I told them, 'The fellow who killed that man is gone. I'm a new man. I haven't killed anybody, don't want to kill anybody, and am not going to kill anybody.'"

He got out on parole, blessed be God! He came here to school, graduated, and is out in the ministry today. We had him preach, and you could tell the anointing of God was on him. That's what the life of God will do for you. He's no longer a criminal.

I remember a dear sister down in Beaumont, Texas. She was an ordained Assemblies of God minister and was always interested in those who were down and out. When she was just a young woman in her 30s (she is now with the Lord), she would go down in a red-light district and win those girls to Jesus. She'd get them saved. She would take them home with her, dress them up, and get them jobs.

She told my wife and me about one of them, a lovely girl. This girl had spent two years at a university, but she got off on the wrong foot and ended up down there.

This sister got her saved and filled with the Spirit; she got her a good job and got her going to church. She was a beautiful girl. A businessman in the city and in the church fell in love with her and wanted to marry her. But she was ashamed of her past, so she left Beaumont and went to another town in Texas. She said, "Don't tell him where I went. I'm ashamed to tell him my past."

He came knocking on this sister's door, crying, and said, "Where did she go? I'm in love with her."

"Come in," she said. "I want to tell you — she is ashamed of her past. I dug her out of the red-light district. She was a prostitute."

He said, "That makes no difference. She is a beautiful child of God and a beautiful woman. I love her. Tell me where she is. I'll go get her. I'll sell my business here and we'll move somewhere else."

So he went and got her and married her. They sold his business and moved to another city. This sister said, "Every Christmas I get a card from them. Twenty-five years have come and gone, and here's what her husband wrote: 'Thank you for digging this jewel out for me 25 years ago. We have had 25 years of bliss; a beautiful marriage. Thank you so much. Thank you for rescuing her for me. I love her so. After 25 years, I believe I love her more now than I did then. Our home is so beautiful. Our children are so beautiful. We're in church and we love the Lord.'"

She said, "I get several cards like that from men, thanking me." Bless God, the life of God changes you!

No case is incurable. This eternal life will destroy the cause of friction in homes and in every department of life. It eliminates selfishness, and there's a new kind of love as well as a new kind of life that comes into man.

How The Life of God Changed Me

I can remember when I was born again as a Baptist boy on the bed of sickness, on April 22, 1933, Saturday night at 20 minutes until 8:00 p.m. in the south bedroom of 405 North College Street in the city of McKinney, Texas. Because I had grown up sick and not able to take care of myself, even the girls could whip me. If I exerted too much energy, my heart wouldn't beat right and I would pass out and fall on the ground.

Our home was broken because my daddy left. As a youngster, I told everybody I met, "When I get grown I'm going to kill him." And I assuredly would have done just that. But something came into me that changed me. Something came into my spirit that made me a new man. It was the life and nature of God that changed me.

After spending 16 months on the bed of sickness, I was healed August 8, 1934, by the power of God through faith and prayer.

Then I went back to high school. I had completed two years before I became bedfast. In September 1934, I went back after missing a year. But I got ahold of something. I realize now that I was unconsciously led by the Holy Spirit. There were two scriptures that I told the Lord about every morning as I walked down the street to school, and sometimes I would read them before I went to school.

First I would read John 1:4, *"In him was life; and the life was the light of men."* And I'd say, "I've got the life of God in me. The nature of God is in me. The wisdom of God is in me."

I didn't know anything about the confession of faith. I never had heard anything like that, but my spirit impelled me to say it, so I would say it. Second Corinthians 5:17 was also a favorite scripture of mine: *"Therefore if any man be in Christ, he is a new creature: old things are passed away; behold, all things are become new."*

I told everybody I met that I was a new creature. Some of the boys would talk and laugh about certain things we used to do. They would say, "Don't you remember that? You were in on it." I would say, "The fellow who was with you boys that night is dead. The real man is living on the inside of me now; I've been born again and I'm a new creature!"

I would stop people on the street and tell them, "I am a new creature." They would say, "What's that?" I'd start preaching and before you knew it, I'd have a crowd right on the street.

From the book of Daniel, I either quoted or read this to the Lord and made my confession on it:

DANIEL 1:3-20
3   And the king spake unto Ashpenaz the master of his eunuchs, that he should bring certain of the children of Israel, and of the king's seed, and of the princes;
4   Children in whom was no blemish, but well favoured, and skilful in all wisdom, and cunning in knowledge, and understanding science, and such as had ability in them to stand in the king's palace, and whom they might teach the learning and the tongue of the Chaldeans.
5   And the king appointed them a daily provision of the king's meat, and of the wine which he drank: so nourishing them three years, that at the end thereof they might stand before the king.
6   Now among these were of the children of Judah, Daniel, Hananiah, Mishael, and Azariah:
7   Unto whom the prince of the eunuchs gave names: for he gave unto Daniel the name of Belteshazzar; and to Hananiah, of Shadrach; and to

Mishael, of Meshach; and to Azariah, of Abednego.

8   But Daniel purposed in his heart that he would not defile himself with the portion of the king's meat, nor with the wine which he drank: therefore he requested of the prince of the eunuchs that he might not defile himself.

9   Now God had brought Daniel into favour and tender love with the prince of the eunuchs.

10 And the prince of the eunuchs said unto Daniel, I fear my lord the king, who hath appointed your meat and your drink: for why should he see your faces worse liking than the children which are of your sort? then shall ye make me endanger my head to the king.

11 Then said Daniel to Melzar, whom the prince of the eunuchs had set over Daniel, Hananiah, Mishael, and Azariah,

12 Prove thy servants, I beseech thee, ten days; and let them give us pulse to eat, and water to drink.

13 Then let our countenances be looked upon before thee, and the countenance of the children that eat of the portion of the king's meat: and as thou seest, deal with thy servants.

14 So he consented to them in this matter, and proved them ten days.

15 And at the end of ten days their countenances appeared fairer and fatter in flesh than all the children which did eat the portion of the king's meat.

16 Thus Melzar took away the portion of their meat, and the wine that they should drink; and gave them pulse.

17 As for these four children, God gave them knowledge and skill in all learning and wisdom: and Daniel had understanding in all visions and dreams.

18 Now at the end of the days that the king had

**said he should bring them in, then the prince of
the eunuchs brought them in before Nebuchadnez-
zar.**
**19 And the king communed with them; and among
them all was found none like Daniel, Hananiah,
Mishael, and Azariah: therefore stood they before
the king.**
**20 And in all matters of wisdom and understand-
ing, that the king inquired of them, he found them
ten times better than all the magicians and
astrologers that were in all his realm.**

Who did that? God did. God gave His children wisdom. I reminded God of what He did back there by giving that to them. That God is in me now. Eternal life is
His nature.

I would say every morning, "I have the nature of
God, the life of God, and the wisdom of God in me." If
somebody asked me I would tell them. They thought I
was a nut, but I would tell them this as we walked
down the street to school. Sometimes a bunch of us took
up a whole street; there was not a lot of traffic. I would
tell them about it.

I would pray, "Daniel had favor with the prince of
the eunuchs (we would call him the dean of the college).
God, give me favor with every teacher; thank you for it.
It is mine. Now impart to me, because I've got the life of
God and the nature of God in me, more wisdom than all
the rest of the class. Let me be ten times better off than
the rest of the class."

I wasn't bragging on me; I was bragging on what He
gave me. I stood at the head of the class. I was the only

one who made a "straight-A" report card.

In fact, in one of our classes, I was the only one who made an "A." Nobody else made anything higher than a "C."

I could read a chapter of a history book (they tested me to see), put the book down, and get up and recite the chapter word for word.

I didn't do that because I had developed my memory. I didn't know a thing in the world about memorization. I did that because I looked to my spirit.

We never have developed our human spirits. We never have walked in the light of what we have.

One of the greatest miracles I have ever seen along these lines happened in a church I pastored. One of my Sunday school teachers told me concerning her oldest child, O , "I sent her to school seven years in the first grade. She couldn't even learn to write her name. The school authorities asked me if I would take her out of school. She never got out of the first grade."

O was a big 14-year-old girl playing with little 7-year-olds, so her mother had to take her out of school.

They had no state school (we're talking about the 1930s, the Depression Days). They had no special classes. The only kind of school they had in Texas was one for feebleminded children. She didn't even qualify for that.

In church O acted like a 3 or 4 year old; she had about that kind of mentality. If she happened not to be sitting with her mother and wanted to get up where her mother was, she would actually get down and scoot along on her stomach under the pews to get up front. When she would get there (usually there was no one on that pew except her mother), she would stretch out like a kid and go to sleep.

One night O went up to the altar (nobody asked her to go) during a revival and knelt along with the others. There she received eternal life and the nature of God. Instantly there was a drastic change!

Before, she wouldn't bathe. If she got neglected for a short period of time, just like a little child, her appearance would be pitiful. She would come to church looking like she hadn't combed her hair in a month; it looked like the rats had slept in it! And what clothes she had were just hanging on her.

But overnight, the very next night, O came in, sat down, and acted as intelligent as any 18-year-old young lady would. Her hair was fixed, she was dressed up, and she looked nice.

You could hardly believe what you saw. The Life of God changed her. It increased the girl's mentality 90 percent overnight!

This was during the beginning of World War II. O went away to visit some relatives, and while she was there she acted so nice and looked so nice that a neighboring farm boy asked her for a date.

She had never had a date in her life. But he began to date her and like her; and she began to like him. They did hurry it up a bit, because he got drafted, but he asked her to marry him. She took him up on it.

He eventually was sent over to the European theater of warfare, not knowing she couldn't even write him a letter.

O stayed with his mother. When he found out she didn't know how to write, he wrote to his mother and said, "Momma, teach her to write. Teach her to write, 'I love you.' I would rather get a letter from her that said, 'I love you,' signed by her, than for you to write several pages of what she told you to write."

So her mother-in-law taught O to write. Then she came back to live with her mother.

I remember her mother said to me one night, "Brother Hagin, I want to show you an eight-page letter O has written her husband by herself." I read the letter. She told him how much she loved him, and then talked about some business. To tell the truth, it was better than some letters I have read from college graduates. I only saw two words misspelled. It was a good letter.

O told him, "I'm saving our money (because she was getting an allotment). I'm paying my tithes." And she was. You could stop to take up an offering on something and she had already paid her tithes to the church. She would always say, "Brother Hagin, I'll give." She would be the first one to give.

You get the nature of God in you and it changes you.

O told her husband, "I'm putting our money in savings, drawing interest, so when you get out maybe we'll have enough to buy a farm." He was a farm boy and only had about a fifth-grade education himself, so she thought maybe he would want to farm.

Where did O get all that wisdom? From the life of God inside her.

Her younger sister was married to a boy in the Navy. She had the highest IQ of anyone in school, and she had gotten saved, too, but she didn't walk in the light of what she had.

The light is the life of man. But you've got to walk in the light of life for it to benefit you. She splurged her money. Her husband was coming home on furlough and she said to her older sister, "Don't you tell him how much money you've got," because she didn't save a dime.

We left that church before the war was over and went into the evangelistic field. I heard that the older sister's husband had come back and decided he wanted to go into construction work instead of farming. He used the money his wife had saved to buy some gravel trucks. They prospered in their business.

Then I heard he was killed in a truck accident. In the process of time, I got back there and was talking to the church secretary.

I asked, "Whatever happened to that girl?"

She took me by the arm and led me out on the front porch. She said, "You knew that her husband was killed in a truck accident?"

I said, "Yes."

She said, "Well, because of the business, he was heavily insured, and O received several hundreds of thousands of dollars of insurance money." She pointed and said, "See that addition?" I could see a number of new houses. The secretary said, "O is building that addition to the city. She handles all her own money; she is her own financier, her own contractor."

And she said, "Every Sunday morning O pays her tithes; she puts all of her offerings into the church. She is always on the front pew with her three children. They're the best dressed, cleanest, most manicured children in the church. And they're the best-behaved children in the church."

That is one of the greatest miracles I have ever seen. Receiving eternal life and walking in the light of it was what made the difference.

Seeing that, I began to notice something back there as a boy preacher. I saw a truth about eternal life. I began to make predictions on how people's children would turn out. I hit it one hundred percent. People can have eternal life, but if they're not walking in the light of it, their children won't turn out right.

My children turned out exactly like I predicted they would. Not only that, but babies born to members of my church who had this life turned out just like I said they would — every single one of them.

Thank God, I learned as a teenager to remind the Lord of Daniel every day. God gave Daniel and the three other children knowledge and skill, because God knows everything.

I would also read the first chapter of John nearly every day, *"In him* [Jesus] *was life; and the life was the light of men"* (John 1:4). I didn't have a Greek concordance then, but I would say, "That life is in me."

You see, the Spirit of God was leading me right. You talk about being led! I would make that confession every day as we went to school. I would say, "The life of God is in me. The life of God is in me. That life is the light."

I knew light stood for development. It was the development of me. It was developing my spirit. It was developing my mentality. I would say, "I've got God in me! I've got God's wisdom in me. I've got God's life in me. I've got God's power in me."

There shouldn't be any failures in us unless we while our time away, not knowing what we've got and not confessing it. Begin to confess, "This life is mine, praise God! It is in me and it is working!" Thank God, it will work.

Walking in the Light of Life

We must learn how to walk in the light of eternal life to enjoy the fullness and the reality of it. Sometimes we think if we have something in the spiritual realm, it should work automatically. It doesn't. In the natural that's even true. You can have something in the natural and not know you have it and it won't do you any good. Yes, it's in your possession, but if you don't know it, it won't do you any good.

For example, back in 1947, I was saving a little money to buy my wife a Christmas present. I started with a $20 bill. I had a secret pocket in my billfold, so I put the bill back there. And I forgot about it.

The last church I pastored was in the oil fields of East Texas. I got out there doing some business and ran out of gasoline. I didn't have a credit card or anything to buy gas with. So I had to call one of the deacons to come get me and bring some gasoline. He came and got me.

Some time later I was going through my billfold and found the $20 bill. I happened to look into that secret pocket and there it was.

For a moment I was astounded. I thought, *Where did that come from? Maybe God put money into my bill- fold.* Then it dawned on me I had put it in there earlier.

You can't say I didn't have the money. You could fill up your gas tank in those days for $4 or $5, so I could have filled up my gas tank four or five times.

I had the money, but it didn't do me any good because I didn't know I had it. That's so naturally and that's so spiritually. When it comes to spiritual things, people think, "If you've got it, you've got it."

No, that's the reason God gave us His Word — so we would take time to find out what we have and then walk in the light of it. You can have eternal life and not know what it really is. You can know you are saved and say, "Well, I'm a Christian. Thank God, I'm saved." And you'll go to Heaven when you die.

But you won't enjoy the reality of eternal Life in *this* life because you don't know what it is, or what it is sup- posed to do for you. We have never majored on this as we should.

Chapter 3
Let Zoe Dominate You

*Always bearing about in the body the dying
of the Lord Jesus, that the life also of Jesus
might be made manifest in our body.*

*For we which live are alway delivered unto
death for Jesus' sake, that the life also of Jesus
might be made manifest in our mortal flesh.*

— 2 Corinthians 4:10,11

The Apostle Paul talks here about the life of God in
our spirits being manifested in our bodies. He is not
talking about the Resurrection, but about something
that happens in this life.

*I'm convinced that if one learns how to walk in the
light of life, and lets that life dominate him, he will live
to a great age (if Jesus tarries).* I know the outward man
is decaying, all right, but this life can be made manifest
in our mortal flesh.

One day a Jewish lawyer came to Jesus and said,
*". . . Good Master, what good thing shall I do, that I
may have eternal life?"* (Matt. 19:16).

This rich young man who came to Jesus represented
the most zealous branch of the family of Abraham, the
children of promise and of the covenant. Yet he knew he
did not have the one thing above all other things that
made him right with God. On the great Day of Atone-

25

ment, when his sins were forgiven, he went away with the consciousness of the fact that something had not been made right in his life.

The hunger was still unsatisfied. The craving on the inside of him was still unmet. He wanted and needed something in his nature that seemed to have been lost somewhere, and he felt his lack. It was something he knew would round out and complete his joy and his longing.

What was it? It was something greater than atonement. It was something greater than justification under the Law. It was something greater than mere forgiveness. The thing he craved is majored on in the Gospel of John.

It is a single word, and this word is the key to the Gospel of John. It is the word that unlocks the divine side of the plan of redemption. It is the biggest word of the Gospel. It is the word that stands for the whole heart teaching of the Gospel of the grace of God. It is the word "life."

Christianity is that divine act which changes a man from the family of Satan to the family of God instantly.

Charles G. Finney would go into a city, and sometimes the whole city would be converted. Many people said his conversions would not last because they were too quick — too instantaneous.

But a greater percentage of Finney's converts stayed saved than any group since the days of the Apostle Paul.

It is a historical fact that 70 to 80 percent of all of Finney's converts were kept. In no other revival is that true, not even in the great Pentecostal revival. Finney taught an instant conversion, because that's what the Word of God teaches.

Let's look at the nature of eternal life.

JOHN 5:26
26 For as the Father hath life in himself; so hath he given to the Son to have life in himself.

Remember, the Greek word for life is *zoe*. "For as the Father has *zoe* in Himself; so has He given to the Son to have *zoe* in Himself."

Then eternal life is the nature of God. It is the being or substance of God.

We are told in Second Peter 1:4, *"Whereby are given unto us exceeding great and precious promises: that by these ye might be partakers of the divine nature [God's nature], having escaped the corruption that is in the world through lust."*

The corruption from which we escaped is spiritual death, the satanic nature. We are made partakers of the divine nature — the nature of God — the life of God.

We read in Ephesians 2:1, *"And you hath he quickened, who were dead in trespasses and sins."*

And in John 5:24 Jesus said, *"Verily, verily, I say unto you, He that heareth my word, and believeth on him that sent me, hath everlasting life, and shall not come into condemnation; but is passed from death unto life."*

You've got life *now*. You're not going to get it when you get to Heaven. Thank God, you have it now.

John also tells us in First John 3:14, *"We know that we have passed from death unto life, because we love the brethren. He that loveth not his brother abideth in death."*

From these scriptures we see that eternal life is the nature of God and that to become a child of God means we become partakers of the divine nature — eternal life.

When we receive eternal life, the satanic nature passes out of us. I'm not talking about the satanic nature passing out of our flesh. I'm talking about the spirit — the real you — the man on the inside.

Spiritual death gave man physical death or mortality for his body. But the new birth gives eternal life to the spirit of man now and the promise of immortality for our physical bodies at the return of the Lord Jesus Christ.

It is interesting to note how we can help others receive this life.

JOHN 20:30,31
30 And many other signs truly did Jesus in the presence of his disciples, which are not written in this book:
31 But these are written, that ye might believe that Jesus is the Christ, the Son of God; and that believing ye might have life through his name.

John said Jesus did a great many things that are not recorded in the Gospels. But he recorded these things for this purpose: *". . . that ye might believe that Jesus is the Christ, the Son of God; and that believing ye might have life through his name."*

The object, then, is that we might have eternal life. The first step is to read what is written in the Gospels that we may know that Jesus is the Son of God. For since He is the Son of God, He has made spiritual life available to spiritually dead men. In the Epistles, Paul tells us:

1 CORINTHIANS 15:3,4
3   For I delivered unto you first of all that which I also received, how that Christ died for our sins according to the scriptures;
4   And that he was buried, and that he rose again the third day according to the scriptures.

Until we know this, seeking eternal life will be in vain. But having satisfied our intellects that Jesus is the Son of God, that He died for our sins according to the Scriptures, that He rose again according to the Scriptures — then we can take the next step. John 1:12 says, *"But as many as received him, to them gave he power to become the sons of God, even to them that believe on his name."*

Receiving Jesus is an act of the will of man, acting on the Word. You know that you're without a Savior, without an approach to God, without eternal life; and you just look up to God and say, "I know that."

But it is not enough just to take Jesus as your Savior. You also must acknowledge His lordship over your life. The reason for this is obvious.

We had been the servants of the devil. We had belonged to the kingdom or the country of the devil. Now we want to leave that country and come into God's country and become naturalized citizens.

But before we can do this, we must swear allegiance to the new fatherland, so to speak, and make our absolute, unconditional break with the old fatherland.

So we must confess Jesus as Lord, as the new ruler of our heart life as well as our intellectual life.

One of the difficulties that confronts people is that they wish to have Jesus as Savior, but not as Lord. Many people want Him as their Savior from hell, but they don't want Him as their ruler on earth.

I've heard ministers of the gospel, even Full Gospel ministers, say they were afraid to make Jesus Lord of their lives.

I heard one say, "I was afraid He might send me off to be a missionary. I preached for years, and Jesus really wasn't my Lord." (That's a sad commentary, but it can be so.)

I heard a well-known evangelist say, "When I made Jesus Lord of my life (and I preached for years before I made Him Lord), my life took on a supernatural aspect that it never had before."

Many things have happened to Christians because they didn't let Jesus be Lord. Many marriages have been entered into that were all wrong because folks didn't take time to see what Jesus had to say about it and let Him be Lord.

One time I heard a preacher telling about Jesus on the Sea of Galilee. Jesus was on the boat with His disciples in the storm when Jesus said to them, ". . . *Peace, be still . . .*" (Mark 4:39).

The Bible says there was a great calm. This preacher remarked, "No matter what is going on in a church service, if you want there to be a great calm, just start talking about money, people's children, or the home and marriage, and there will be a great calm."

Too many times that's absolutely the truth. We get into trouble in these areas because we don't listen to what the Lord has to say about them. The Bible says, *"The spirit of man is the candle of the Lord, searching all the inward parts of the belly"* (Prov. 20:27).

I remember in one church I pastored there was a beautiful Christian woman. She was one of the most spiritual persons I have ever met. I've been in the ministry and known pastors and pastors' wives, and evangelists and evangelists' wives, and this woman was more spiritual than any preacher I knew.

She knew God. She knew how to pray. She knew how to touch God. She had the gifts of the Spirit operating in her life. But I don't care how spiritual you are. I don't care how many gifts of the Spirit you have operating in your life. I don't care how well you know how to get ahold of God, if you don't make and keep Jesus as Lord of your life, you can get into trouble.

He's the living Word. God has given us the written Word to unveil the living Word to us.

Give the Word of God, the New Testament, primarily, first place in your life. By so doing, you are putting Jesus first.

Let this Word govern you life. Let this Word be the Lord of your life. Let the Word have dominion over you.

By so doing, you are letting Jesus dominate you.

Now this dear woman was the finest Christian in the church. There was no one who was more dependable or a better prayer warrior. We pastored there, moved away, and God sent us back several years later.

When we returned we heard this woman had remarried, and we were glad about it. She was about 55 years of age and her first husband was dead.

One of her grown, married daughters was in the church, and she came over to help us unpack and straighten up the parsonage. My wife asked her about her mother's marriage.

A look of concern came across the girl's face.

She said, "Brother and Sister Hagin, I think Momma missed God." Instantly we were greatly concerned. We knew this woman was a precious woman of God.

She said her mother had taken a job in another city. She had started going with a certain gentleman and brought him home for the children to meet.

"I could see she was serious with this fellow," the girl explained. "I asked, 'Momma, you're not about to marry that guy, are you?'

"She said, 'I most certainly am.' I said, 'We children don't care if you are married; that's fine. But the Bible says only to be married in the Lord, not to be unequally yoked together with unbelievers' [2 Cor. 6:14].

"She said he was a church member. But I said, 'Momma, you've been around long enough; you know that every church member is not saved. In fact, I don't want to be the judge, but there are some people who are members of our Full Gospel church who are not saved. It's not church membership that saves you — it's being born again — receiving eternal life.

"'Besides that, I don't want to judge him. I don't want you to think I'm opposing this, and I've never seen him until today, but there's something about him that's not right. He looks to me like an old beer guzzler.'

"Momma said, 'Well, he does drink some. But he said he would quit if I would marry him.'"

You know, these older girls are just as easily fooled as the young ones are. Whether you're old, young, or middle aged, if he won't quit before you marry him, he won't quit after you marry him.

This dear woman was such a spiritual woman, a fine Christian, but I don't care how wonderful you are, how spiritual you are, how far advanced you are — you are not immune to being misled if you get away from the Bible.

So this girl said to her mother, "Now Momma, you know better than that."

Her mother said, "I'm going to fast and pray about it; and I'm going to put out a fleece before the Lord."

Her daughter said, "There's no use putting out a fleece. There's no need fasting and praying.

"The Bible has already said not to be unequally yoked together with unbelievers. The Bible has already said to be married only in the Lord. We don't care if you are married, but find somebody of equal spiritual experience to build a life with."

This woman fasted, prayed, and put out a fleece. Her fleece indicated she should go ahead and marry the fellow, so she married him.

Somewhere along the way, Jesus ceased to dominate her life. The Word was no longer dominant in her life.

A day or so later my wife happened to look down the street and say to me, "That looks like Sister So-and-So."

I said, "No, it couldn't be, because she's living in another city 45 miles from here."

We watched, though, and as she got closer we recognized it was her. As she got to the edge of our yard, we could see something was wrong. Her eye was black, and her nose was large and swollen. Her face was beaten up. By the time she hit the parsonage porch, she was squalling and bawling like a baby. She hugged my wife and me.

We got her into the parsonage — into the living room — and finally got her quieted down enough to find out what happened.

She told us what her husband had done. On the way home from work about ten days before, he had stopped off for something to drink, and by the time he got home he had been pretty well "lit up."

She said something he didn't particularly like, so he hit her right in the middle of her face, knocked her down, jumped on top of her, and started beating her in the face.

He almost beat her to death. He tore her clothes nearly off. She had to run out of the house half-clothed and catch a streetcar to go across the city to her daughter's house. Afterward, the woman was bedfast for ten days.

"I'll tell you one thing," she said. "When I get up to Heaven, I've got something to ask the Lord. I'm going to ask Him why He put this off on me."

I said, "Now Sister, you know me — I've pastored you before — and I'm not trying to be a smart aleck, but you won't have to wait until you get to Heaven. If you'll just ask me, I'll tell you now.

"God didn't put that off on you. You wanted that old rascal and you got him! You've got him on your hands now. What are you going to do with him?"

Well, that poor woman had a hard time. I'm sure — I know beyond a shadow of a doubt — that it shortened her life. She could have lived longer. Thank God, she did get him saved, and he died saved — he barely made it in. But I'm sure of this one thing — all the trouble and concern shortened her life.

We can make some choices for ourselves in life, but it is always better to choose God's best. It is always better to go with God. It is always better to walk in the light of life.

Chapter 4
Ruling and Reigning In Union With God

For if by one man's offence death reigned by one; much more they which receive abundance of grace and of the gift of righteousness shall reign in life by one, Jesus Christ.

— Romans 5:17

What does this verse mean? It means that every one of us who has been born again and has received the life of God has come into a kingly state. We are accepted by God to reign as kings in the realm of life.

We are no longer servants in the realm of spiritual death, but we have passed out of death, Satan's realm, into the realm of the supernatural or the heavenlies.

Man was never made to be a slave. He was made to reign as a king under God. That kingly being was created in the image and likeness of God.

He was created on terms of equality with God, and he could stand in God's presence without any consciousness of inferiority.

Notice Psalm 8:4,5: *"What is man, that thou art mindful of him? and the son of man, that thou visitest him? For thou hast made him a little lower than the angels, and hast crowned him with glory and honour."*

In some translations there is a number or letter by the word "angels" in this text. If you look in the margin you'll find that the Hebrew word here is *Elohim* — the same word or name for God. The Hebrew Bible actually says (talking about man), *"Thou hast made him a little lower than God."*

That means God has made us as much like Himself as possible. He made us in His image. He made us in His likeness. He made us the same class of being that He is Himself. He made Adam with an intellect of such caliber that he could name every animal, vegetable, and fruit, and give them names that would describe their characteristics. When God could do that with man, man belonged to the realm of God.

In the first five chapters of Genesis, *Elohim* is the name for God. Man, then, was made in the likeness of *Elohim. He was made with the life of God in him.*

GENESIS 2:7
7 And the Lord God formed man of the dust of the ground, and breathed into his nostrils the breath of life; and man became a living soul.

The Hebrew word translated "breath" is the same word translated "spirit" all through the Old Testament.

God took something of Himself, which was spirit, the life of God, and put it into man. You see that life manifested in man. You see it in his spirit and soul. You see it in his body, even after he had died spiritually.

God made man His understudy, so to speak. He made him king, to rule over everything that had life.

Man was master. Man lived in the realm of God.

God is a faith God. All He had to do was simply say,
". . . *Let there be light . . .*" (Gen. 1:3), and there was
light. God created everything except man by speaking it
into existence. He's a faith God.

Now God made man a faith man, because man
belongs to God's class. A faith man lives in the creative
realm of God. This revelation brings an end to the
weakness message!

Man lost his place by high treason against God. He
lost his dominion over all the works of God's hands. He
lost his dominion in the fall. With the fall went his
dominion over his spirit and soul.

But my friends, if one is a thinker or a student of
history, one knows universal man has ever yearned for
the return of his lost dominion.

Here's one of the most tremendous facts we have to
face: There never has been a primitive people found
upon the face of the earth who have not yet yearned for
dominion.

Not a single primitive people has been found who
did not have a golden past where they had dominion,
and a golden future where dominion was going to be
restored. That is the tradition of universal man.

The reason for that is, man was created to have
dominion. Man has shrunk from bondage. Man has
rebelled against it. Man has yearned to gain mastery
over physical loss, over mind loss, and over the loss of
the spirit.

This age-old desire to gain man's lost dominion is seen in his offerings, in his drinking blood, and in the priesthoods he has appointed.

If you study history, you'll find that human blood was never actually desirable to any people. Why did they drink it? They drank it to be like God. They drank it that they might become eternal or immortal. The desire for immortality in the physical realm lies in the heart of universal man. And for that reason, men drank it.

They would take an animal or another man and make a sacrifice upon the altar of their god or gods. And when they did, they believed that the offering became identified with God.

They said, "If we drink the blood of the man or the animal, we drink the blood of God. And if we drink enough of it, we'll be God."

Actually, that's not too far removed from the Communion table. Why do you suppose that kind of thinking is in the hearts and minds of even primitive people the world around?

You see, it all dates back to the beginning. Remember the first two offsprings of Adam and Eve, Cain and Abel? Remember that they both brought an offering to God and one was rejected while the other was received?

The offering that was received — Abel's — was an offering of blood, while the one that was rejected — Cain's — was an offering of fruits and vegetables.

So you see, this kind of thinking has filtered down even through primitive people, that blood has something to do with regaining mastery and dominion upon the earth.

And thank God it does! Without the shedding of blood there is no remission of sins. When Jesus instituted the Lord's Supper He said:

MATTHEW 26:26-28
26 ... Take, eat; this is my body.
27 And he took the cup, and gave thanks, and gave it to them, saying, Drink ye all of it;
28 For this is my blood of the new testament, which is shed for many for the remission of sins.

He signified that when we eat that bread and drink that cup, we partake of Him. We are identified with God. We are actually one with Him.

Many ancients became cannibals, not because they loved human blood, but because they believed if they could eat flesh and drink blood they would be like God.

This faith of universal man, reaching God-ward, cried out to God to make union with Him a possibility. Man believed union with God would give him dominion. And it will.

Man hates defeat. He wants to conquer death. He dreams of immortality and fears death and disease.

Man believed that somehow God would give him this lost dominion. Now you can understand it was this universal knowledge, the universal cry of man for union with Deity, that caused the Incarnation.

So the Lord Jesus Christ came into this world. He was God incarnated in the flesh.

Jesus was God and man in union. He was first a divine being.

JOHN 1:1
1 In the beginning was the Word, and the Word was with God, and the Word was God.

But He came and dwelt among us.

JOHN 1:14
14 And the Word was made flesh, and dwelt among us.

He was God incarnate in the flesh. So Jesus was a divine-human being. Now on the grounds of what the Lord Jesus Christ did (that is, His substitutionary sacrifice), God is able to redeem us from our sins.

He is able to redeem us from spiritual death. He is able to impart to us His very nature. He is able to give us eternal life, His very own life. He is able to take us into His own family, so that we can call Him Father.

Paul said, ". . . *I bow my knees unto the Father of our Lord Jesus Christ. Of whom the whole family in heaven and earth is named*" (Eph. 3:14,15).

You can tell the way some people say "God" that they believe He's some far-off Creature somewhere. No, He's *Father.* He may be "God" to the world, but He's Father to me!

In the new birth, we are brought into vital union with Jesus Christ. All that most people think they have in the new birth is forgiveness of sins. They don't know about being in union with God.

Even many in the great body of Full Gospel people do not fully realize that in the new birth they become one spirit with God (1 Cor. 6:17).

They do not know they are as much sons and daughters of God as Jesus. They only have a hazy concept of what God has done, of what He is to them, and of what they are to God.

The union with Him that God has given through the new birth has bestowed upon us the lost authority we had in the Garden of Eden. And only here or there has a man known it or preached it, or dared to assume it.

No wonder Smith Wigglesworth said, "I'm a thousand times bigger on the inside than I am on the outside." He was realizing that God dwelled within him.

Let's look at a few scriptures so you'll know God is living in you.

> **JOHN 14:15,16**
> **15 If ye love me, keep my commandments.**
> **16 And I will pray the Father, and he shall give you another Comforter, that he may abide with you for ever.**

> **1 CORINTHIANS 3:16**
> **16 Know ye not that ye are the temple of God, and that the Spirit of God dwelleth in you?**

> **1 CORINTHIANS 6:19,20**
> **19 What? know ye not that your body is the temple of the Holy Ghost which is in you, which ye have of God, and ye are not your own?**
> **20 For ye are bought with a price: therefore glo-**

rify God in your body, and in your spirit, which
are God's.

2 CORINTHIANS 6:16
16 And what agreement hath the temple of God
with idols? . . .

Remember that Paul already said in First Corinthians 3:16, *"Know ye not that ye are the temple of God,
and that the Spirit of God dwelleth in you?"* Here he
says it again. He wants to get that point across.

I've got God the Holy Spirit living in me. We've
never even majored on that subject before. We have
been too busy fighting over minor things.

Some of these great Bible truths that will release
us, and enable us to dominate and reign in life have
been left untouched. When you begin to preach on
them, many people in Christendom will sit and look at
you in amazement. I wouldn't have dared suggest these
things if I hadn't had scriptures to back me up.

*He's in me. He's in you. In the new birth, I've come
into vital union with God!*

We are the temple of the living God. Now, let's get a
picture of the living God. Let's go back to the Old Testament and see Him.

The Presence of God (the Jews called it the *shekinah*) was only in the Holy of Holies. At least once a
year, every male in Israel had to present himself at the
Temple that God had Solomon build.

God wasn't dwelling in the Israelites, so they had to
go to where God was. That's the reason we've got a bet-

ter covenant established on better promises (Heb. 8:6).

No one dared approach the Holy of Holies except the High Priest. Others who tried would fall dead on the spot. Only the High Priest, after the blood of innocent animals was shed for the atonement of sin, could enter in.

Many have thought that when Jesus said on the Cross, "It is finished" He was talking about our salvation. No! No! No!

Our salvation wasn't finished when Jesus died. Salvation wasn't complete until He ascended into the heavenly Holy of Holies to obtain eternal redemption for us (*see* Hebrews chapter 9).

When Jesus said "It is finished" on the Cross, He was talking about the Old Covenant being finished. And when He said those words, the curtain that sealed off the Holy of Holies in the Temple was rent in twain — or torn in half — from top to bottom (Mark 15:38).

Flavius Josephus, the Jewish historian, tells us that the curtain was 20 feet high, 40 feet across, and 4 inches thick.

Did you notice the scripture didn't say the curtain was rent in twain from bottom to top? It said from *top to bottom.*

Up there 20 feet in the air, an angel of God, or some heavenly somebody, got hold of the thing and ripped it apart. *That signified that the way into the Holy of Holies, blessed be God, is now open to everybody through the blood of Jesus!*

God moved out of an earth-made, man-made Holy of Holies, and He dwells in us! *He lives in us! You are the temple where the holy shekinah Presence of God dwells.*

We've never mastered that yet. We've thought it *sounded* like it could not be true. But, thank God, it *is* true!

Second Corinthians 6:16 says, *"And what agreement hath the temple of God with idols? for ye are the temple of the living God; as God hath said, I will dwell in them, and walk in them; and I will be their God, and they shall be my people."*

Here are some further facts.

> **1 John 4:1-4**
> **1   Beloved, believe not every spirit, but try the spirits whether they are of God: because many false prophets are gone out into the world.**
> **2   Hereby know ye the Spirit of God: Every spirit that confesseth that Jesus Christ is come in the flesh is of God:**
> **3   And every spirit that confesseth not that Jesus Christ is come in the flesh is not of God: and this is that spirit of antichrist, whereof ye have heard that it should come; and even now already is it in the world.**
> **4   YE ARE OF GOD, little children. . . .**

Because we are of God, because we are born of God, we are sons of God.

> **1 JOHN 3:1,2**
> **1   Behold, what manner of love the Father hath bestowed upon us, that we should be called the sons of God: therefore the world knoweth us not, because it knew him not.**
> **2   Beloved, now are we the sons of God, and it**

doth not yet appear what we shall be: but we
know that, when he shall appear, we shall be like
him; for we shall see him as he is.

1 JOHN 5:1,2
1   Whosoever believeth that Jesus is the Christ is
born of God: and every one that loveth him that
begat loveth him also that is begotten of him.
2   By this we know that we love the children of
God, when we love God, and keep his command-
ments.

Friends, we are sons of God. We are children of God.
We are born of God. We are in the family of God. *We are
in union with God.*

1 JOHN 4:4
4   Ye are of God, little children, and have overcome them: because greater is he that is in you,
than he that is in the world.

It doesn't say we're *going to* overcome them (the
forces of evil), but we *have* overcome them. If we have
overcome one of them, we've overcome *all* of them.

We say, "If I've overcome them, why am I having so
much trouble with them?" *Because you don't know who
you are in Christ!* Because you don't know that you're
supposed to rule over them!

Remember, we're talking about reigning as kings in
life. Satan has been defeated. He's not *going* to be; he
has been defeated. When Jesus walked the earth, He
won every battle with the enemy.

Then, after Jesus had satisfied the claims of justice
on the Cross, He met the devil in the devil's own throne

room, stripped him of his authority and dominion, and rose from the dead victorious.

In Revelation 1:18 Jesus said, *"I am he that liveth, and was dead; and, behold, I am alive for evermore, Amen; and have the keys of hell and of death."* Where did He get them? He got them from Satan; He took the dominion and authority that had been given Satan in the Garden of Eden by Adam.

Now every man and woman who accepts Jesus Christ is identified with Him. He did it for *you*. He did it for *me*. He did it as our Substitute. Satan can holler as much as he wants to. But you withstand him; don't be the least bit afraid of him. Withstand him with the faith of Jesus Christ.

The trouble with a lot of us is we live up there in the *faith* realm, but we've gone down the back stairs in the *reason* realm. Some people are holding onto devilish reasoning. But when Jesus died as our Substitute, we were identified with Him. That is the reason we're over-comers.

EPHESIANS 2:2-6
2 Wherein in time past ye walked according to the course of this world, according to the prince of the power of the air, the spirit that now worketh in the children of disobedience:
3 Among whom also we all had our conversation in times past in the lusts of our flesh, fulfilling the desires of the flesh and of the mind; and were by nature the children of wrath, even as others.
4 But God, who is rich in mercy, for his great love wherewith he loved us,
5 Even when we were dead in sins, hath quick-

> ened [made alive] **us together with Christ, (by grace
> ye are saved;)**
> **6   And hath raised us up together, and made us
> sit together in heavenly places in Christ Jesus.**

When Jesus was made alive, we were made alive!
We are identified with Christ in what He did. So when
are we to reign as kings? During the Millennium? In
"the sweet by and by"? No, *in life!* The potential is
there, and it belongs to you. I'm going to live up to the
full potential of what belongs to me in Christ Jesus.

You're the one who has authority in your life. I don't
have authority in your life. That's the problem — we're
running around trying to find someone else to be king.
I'm not to be king in your life — *you* are to be king in
your own life.

We have failed to realize what Jesus did. We have
failed to realize who we are. We have failed to take
advantage of what belongs to us. And so, when trouble
comes, we become fearful.

But no, blessed be God, here's why we've overcome:
". . . *greater is he that is in you, than he that is in the
world*" (1 John 4:4).

Who is it that is in this world? Satan is the god of
this world. Second Corinthians 4:4 says he is called the
god of this world; he's here. Adam *was* the god of this
world, but he sold out to Satan and Satan became god.
Jesus, however, stripped Satan of that authority. He
gave it back to us.

We've sat around begging for authority, and we had
it all the time! We've sat around waiting for God to do

something, yet He's waiting for *us* to do something.

I will never forget when the Lord appeared to me in a vision in 1952 in the state of Oklahoma. He said, "I'm going to talk to you about the devil, demons, and demon possession."

The whole thing lasted about an hour and a half. Jesus stood before me as I knelt. Suddenly an evil spirit that looked like a monkey jumped up between us and caused a black cloud to appear.

I couldn't see Jesus, but I could hear Him. He kept right on talking. Meanwhile, the spirit threw his arms and legs out and hollered in a shrill voice, "Yakety-yak, yakety-yak, yakety-yak." He kept on acting that way and thoughts ran through my mind faster than machine gun bullets could fire.

I thought, *Dear Lord! I'm missing what Jesus is saying.* Jesus was giving me instructions about dealing with the devil.

I could hear the sound of His voice, but I couldn't distinguish the words because of this "yakety-yak" business. I couldn't see Jesus because the cloud was there.

Then I thought, *Doesn't Jesus know? Doesn't He know I'm not hearing Him? Why doesn't Jesus do something about it? Why does He allow it?*

Aren't those the kinds of questions asked all the time? "Why did God allow it? Why doesn't God do something about it?"

Finally, in desperation, I spoke to the spirit. I said, "I command you to shut up in the Name of Jesus."

When I said that, he hit the floor like a sack of salt: Kerflop. The dark cloud disappeared, and I could see Jesus.

Then Jesus said something that absolutely astonished me; something that upended my theology. (We get so concerned about theology that we miss what the Bible is saying to us.)

Jesus pointed to that little fellow lying there (and not only lying there — he was shaking all over — trembling from head to foot and whining).

Jesus pointed to him and said, "If you hadn't done something about that, I couldn't have."

Listen and reign! Let it slip by you and be in slavery!

In my astonishment, I said, "Lord! I know I misunderstood You. I'm sure I did. You didn't say You *couldn't* — and I pointed to that little fellow lying there still whimpering and shaking all over — You said You *wouldn't*, didn't You?"

Jesus said, "I said (and He pointed to him) if you hadn't done something about that, I *couldn't*."

Now understand "that" doesn't just include the demon; it included the dark cloud that shut off the vision of Jesus and Heaven. It included communication that didn't get through — prayers or whatever.

I said, "Lord, I know something happened to me. You didn't say You *couldn't*; You said You *wouldn't*, didn't You?"

And very emphatically He said, "No! I didn't say I *wouldn't*; I said I *couldn't*."

"Oh, dear Lord," I said. "I can't accept that. It's against everything I ever believed! It's against everything I ever preached!"

I said, "I won't accept any vision unless You can prove it to me from the Bible; particularly the New Testament. You said in Your Word, *'In the mouth of two or three witnesses every word may be established'"* (Matt. 18:16).

Do you think He got angry with me? No, He smiled so sweetly and said, "I'll go you one better; I'll give you four."

He said, "There's no place in the New Testament where the Church or Christian believers are told to pray against the devil. To pray against the devil is to waste your time."

When He said that to me I said, "Dear Lord! I've wasted so much time!"

He said, "The New Testament tells believers themselves to do something about the devil. And if they don't there won't be anything done. I've done all I'm ever going to do about the devil."

That came as a real shock to me. "Now," He said, "I'll give you the four references which proved that. First of all, in Matthew 28, when I arose from the dead, I said, *'All power is given unto me in heaven and in earth'* [Matt. 28:18]. The word 'power' means *authority*."

If you stopped reading right here you'd say, "Why, dear Lord Jesus, You do have authority here on the earth."

But He said, "I immediately delegated My authority on earth to the Church."

MARK 16:15-18
15 . . . Go ye into all the world, and preach the gospel to every creature.
16 He that believeth and is baptized shall be saved; but he that believeth not shall be damned.
17 And these signs shall follow them that believe; In my name shall they cast out devils; they shall speak with new tongues;
18 They shall take up serpents; and if they drink any deadly thing, it shall not hurt them; they shall lay hands on the sick, and they shall recover.

You see, *you are* authorized to do that.

Then Jesus said to me, "Not one single time does any New Testament writer tell you to pray to God or to Me, the Lord Jesus Christ, to do anything about the devil. Every single time they tell *you* to do it. *You're* the one who has authority. *You're* the one who is to rule."

The next reference He gave me was James 4:7: *"Submit yourselves therefore to God. Resist the devil, and he will flee from you."*

Now, as Jesus said, you couldn't do that if you didn't have authority over the devil.

Ephesians 4:27 says, *"Neither give place to the devil."* Jesus quoted that to me, saying, "That simply means, 'Don't let the devil have any place in you.'"

Jesus said, "That means the devil can't take any place in you, unless you let him. That means you've got the authority."

Now let's go back to the vision I saw. Dark clouds sometimes appear on the horizon of our lives, blotting out the light from Heaven that is seeking to shine in. We say, "Why did God permit that to happen to me?"

That darkness, you see, can be an illustration of many things — sickness, problems, any adverse circumstance. We say, "Why did God send this? Why doesn't God do something about it?" Can you understand it? *You're the one who's supposed to do something about it!*

Authority in the Life of Smith Wigglesworth

Smith Wigglesworth once received a telegram urging him to visit a young woman 200 miles from his home. He went there and found her mother and father brokenhearted because their daughter had lost her mind. They said the devil had gotten hold of her.

Silently they led him down a hall and up two flights of stairs. Finally they reached a closed door. The girl's father opened it, swung it back, and pushed Wigglesworth inside.

He said, "I looked in the room and there was a frail little girl, just in her twenties, lying on the floor held down by five grown men."

When the girl saw him, the strength in that frail body was so great (she was empowered by the devil) that she overcame the five men. They couldn't hold her. She tore loose from them, faced Wigglesworth with blazing eyes, and said, "You can't cast me out! You can't cast me out!"

Wigglesworth said, "Jesus can, and He's in me." (He remembered First John 4:4: *"Greater is he that is in you, than he that is in the world."*)

Wigglesworth knew something about being in union with God. He knew something about having the living God in him — Christ in him. "Jesus can," he said, "so come out in the Name of Jesus!"

Thirty-four of them came out and gave their names. The girl's mind was restored, and she walked downstairs and ate her evening meal. Praise God!

The Name of Jesus is greater than the forces of evil. And the Greater One is living in you.

Once I was preaching some of these truths in another state. I remember that a Full Gospel Business Men's chapter president said to me, "Brother Hagin, hearing this makes me feel like I could do anything." I said, "You can; go out and do it!"

A day or two later, a man flew in who was going to speak at several chapters, including this man's chapter. The two of them were driving to a breakfast meeting in another city, and they were traveling quite fast. (The speed limit was about 70 miles per hour then.)

It was not exactly dark and not exactly light — they couldn't see too well.

Suddenly a woman appeared in front of that big Lincoln automobile. The chapter president couldn't possibly stop — he hit her, and her body flew up over the windshield, over the car, and landed back down the highway.

He quickly pulled over to the side of the road. It sounded like they had run into a truck. They knew every bone in her body had to be broken.

This chapter president told me, "I just sat there in shock. A motorist going the other way said he would notify the authorities. The man who was with me ran back to the woman.

A nurse in one of the other cars that stopped said, 'I can't find a pulse beat — she's dead. There's no life in her.'

The ambulance came, and all at once I could hear you preaching, *'Greater is he that is in you, than he that is in the world.'*

Before I knew what I was doing, I climbed out of the car, ran back to the woman, laid hands on her, and commanded her to live in the Name of Jesus."

After the ambulance left for the hospital, the chapter president went on and drove his guest to the speaking engagement.

Afterwards they came back through the same little town where the woman had been taken to the hospital.

Her doctors told the men, "We're going to dismiss her; we can't find a thing wrong with her. She doesn't have a broken bone in her body."

Glory to God! How big is God?

Chapter 5

Reigning Through Righteousness

Some have said, "I don't see anyone reigning."

The reason is, reigning hasn't been proclaimed. God said in the Old Testament, *"My people are destroyed for lack of knowledge . . ."* (Hosea 4:6). He is inferring that if His people possess knowledge of who they are and who God is — if they know their rights, their privileges, and their dominion — they won't be destroyed.

The reason Satan is often able to reign in the lives of Christians is because many times Christians do not realize they have a part to play. The Bible doesn't say Jesus Christ will reign through you; it says you *". . . shall reign in life by one, Jesus Christ"* (Rom. 5:17).

Many people think, "I've left it up to the Lord. He is going to do it." The truth of the matter is, He's left it up to us. What are we supposed to do? Let's find out our authority and our position. We have received "abundance of grace" and "the gift of righteousness." (Rom. 5:17)

We know a great deal about grace (we've heard that preached) and we've sung "Amazing Grace." And thank God for the grace of God. But we've also received "the gift of righteousness."

I don't think the Church as a whole knows what Paul is talking about when he says that. We've heard very little teaching on the subject. It's receiving the abundance of grace and *the gift of righteousness* that enables one to reign.

If you don't know what you've received, you'll be hindered in reigning. What does "the gift of righteousness" mean?

First, it means you're made right with God. It means right-standing with God. We used to sing a song, "Nothing Between My Soul and the Savior." You see, if there's nothing between, righteousness is what made it so.

It wasn't something I did; it was my accepting His provision. If I'm in right-standing with God, then I can't ever be in any better standing with God. That's something we need to get into our spirits.

The Bible talks about growing in faith, but not about growing in righteousness. Paul wrote to the Church at Thessalonica, *". . . your faith groweth exceedingly . . ."* (2 Thess. 1:3).

First Peter 2:2 says, *". . . desire the sincere milk of the word, that ye may grow thereby."* We could quote other scriptures. But nowhere does the Bible talk about *growing* in righteousness; it always calls righteousness a gift.

You'll not have any better standing with God when you get to Heaven than you do now. Did you know that the newborn babe in the kingdom of God has the same standing as an old saint who's been living a separated, holy, sanctified life for 80 years? It's all done through Jesus in the new birth.

We're held back by traditional teaching and "church-ianity." In the denomination I was raised in, we were famous for saying, "I'm so weak and unworthy." We thought we were being humble — we didn't know we were being ignorant!

We thought having a low opinion of ourselves was really being humble. We'd say, "I'll never amount to anything. I'm just a worm of the dust. Poor ol' me; I'm just a sinner saved by grace." That's wrong! I*m* saved by grace, and I *was* a sinner, but I'm no longer a sinner — now I'm a saint! Sometimes you hear Christians say, "I'm going to be a saint." If you're born again, you *are* one already.

We thought we were being humble. And, of course, when we came to pray, we always told God how wretched and miserable we were. We didn't have enough faith to believe God for anything.

Then I received the baptism in the Holy Spirit and spoke with other tongues, got excommunicated by the Baptists, and came over among the Pentecostals. They did know more about the Holy Spirit, but they didn't know some other things. Sometimes they were bound by the same traditions.

It was a custom before every revival to have a week of prayer and fasting. I don't mean we fasted all week, but we'd fast some and go to church and pray every night. One time I listened to some of our praying — and I started laughing. I found out why things didn't work. We thought we'd tell God all week how unworthy we were.

By the time we started revival, we had talked our-selves out of everything. If anybody did come to the altar, we didn't have enough power left to blow the hat off his head!

We'd say, "Lord, just get everything out of the way, so You can bless me." We didn't have sense enough to know that *we* were in the way all the time. When I was a boy on the bed of sickness, I read:

> **JAMES 5:14,15**
> 14 Is any sick among you? let him call for the elders of the church; and let them pray over him, anointing him with oil in the name of the Lord:
> 15 And the prayer of faith shall save the sick, and the Lord shall raise him up; and if he have committed sins, they shall be forgiven him.

The devil said to me, "If you were righteous, you could pray that prayer of faith."

I didn't know what a righteous man was any more than the man in the moon, so I began to study the Scriptures. I saw that Elijah was used as an example of a righteous man praying. I remembered studying about him in Sunday school, and I remembered some of his actions. He reminded me of myself! He was inconsistent. He prayed fire down on Mount Carmel, yet when he was told Jezebel was going to cut his head off, he started running (1 Kings 18:46-19:4).

He ran 18 miles across the plain of Jezreel with the hand of God on him, but then he started running just in fear. He climbed under a juniper tree and said, "Oh, dear God, let me die. I might as well be dead." (Like anyone who has ever said, "I wish I were dead," he didn't really want to die.)

If he'd wanted to die, he could have stayed where he was, and Jezebel would have accommodated him! I identified with Elijah. I thought, *Dear God, how in the world did Elijah qualify as an example of a righteous man?*

Then I began to examine the Old Testament on the subject. Psalm 32 says, *"Blessed is he . . . whose sin is covered. Blessed is the man unto whom the Lord imputeth not iniquity . . ."* (vv. 1,2).

I saw that the blood of the animals of the Old Testament covered men's sin; it made an atonement for them. God didn't attribute the sin to men; He gave them righteousness.

I got into the New Testament and found that the blood of Jesus does not *cover* sins. The New Testament says, *"Unto him that loved us, and WASHED us from our sins in his own blood"* (Rev. 1:5).

I found in Second Corinthians 5:17, *"Therefore if any man be in Christ, he is a new creature."* I knew immediately God didn't make any unrighteous new creature. I knew God didn't make a new creature who could not stand in His Presence.

We felt when we came into the Presence of God we should get down and crawl on our stomachs. Or we felt we should hang around the front door of Heaven, or sit on the curbstone in front of our mansion and cry until God opened the door and invited us in.

Or we felt we should come to the back door of Heaven like a tramp and try to talk God into giving us a handout. We'd sing, "Here I wander like a beggar through the heat and cold . . . poor ol' me."

But I read Hebrews 4:16: *"Let us therefore come boldly unto the throne of grace, that we may obtain mercy, and find grace to help in time of need."* I got rid of my "spiritual inferiority complex," as I call it.

Of course, the devil was right there to try to stop my faith from working. He said, "Yeah, God made you a righteous creature all right, but remember when you got mad and knocked your food tray off your bed? It was *after* you were born again that you did wrong."

I got back into the Word. I got ahold of that verse in First John 2:1 that says, *"My little children, these things write I unto you, that ye sin not. And if any man sin, we have an advocate with the Father, Jesus Christ the righteous."*

An advocate is a lawyer, one who pleads your case. Jesus Christ the Righteous is my standing, even if I've erred. I've got One up there who's going to plead my case. He's the Advocate of the Christian who has sinned.

Somebody said, "I don't like to hear you say that. I believe in living above sin." Well, I do too. I've never seen anybody do it, but I still believe in it.

Now look at First John 2:2, *"And he* [Jesus Christ the Righteous] *is the propitiation for our sins: and not for ours only, but also for the sins of the whole world."*

Notice John is writing about Christians and their sin, but he is not encouraging them to sin. He already said, *". . . write I unto you, that ye sin not."*

I've had people tell me that this kind of preaching will give people a license to sin. But I tell them, "No,

I'm not going to give them a license to sin; they'll do enough sinning without a license."

If you're really born again, you don't want to sin anyway. If you want to sin, there's something wrong with you. D. L. Moody gave this illustration in one of his sermons.

A young lady in Chicago said to him, "Mr. Moody, I want to be saved, but I can't give up dancing." Mr. Moody preached against worldly dancing. (Any Christian is against it.)

Mr. Moody, being wise, said, "Well, young lady, you just come right into the inquiry room (we'd call it a prayer room) and give your heart and life to the Lord Jesus Christ, and then you can dance all you want to."

She took him at his word, went into the room, and got saved. Four or five days later she met him on the street. She stopped, smiled, shook hands with him and said, "Mr. Moody, I see what you're talking about now. The 'want-to' is gone."

I don't know about you, but I'm "lying" all I want to; I'm "stealing" all I want to; I'm "cussing" all I want to. I'm "hating" all I want to; I'm "hating" everybody I want to hate. No, I'm not hating anybody; there is no hate in me. The "want-to" is gone. If you're really born again, the man on the inside doesn't want to do wrong.

I remember the first time I missed it after I was born again. It wasn't something serious, but it was wrong, and my conscience smote me. I felt so bad. I hadn't wanted to do wrong. I hadn't wanted to miss it or to fail. But, thank God, provision has been made for us.

If I sin and lose my sense of righteousness, blessed be God, He's up there and He's righteous. Jesus goes into the throne room of God and says, "I took his place; I shed My blood for him."

One time when I was younger, I read the verse, ". . . *The effectual fervent prayer of a righteous man availeth much*" (James 5:16), I wrote in red ink beside the verse, "If I ever get to be righteous, then when it comes to praying, I'll be a whiz."

When I found out who I was in Christ — that I was the righteousness of God in Christ — I wrote in red ink beside that verse, "I'm a whiz when it comes to praying." And I've been a whiz ever since then! You're a whiz, too, if you only knew it.

Yes, I'm a whiz when it comes to praying. Now what do I mean by that? I mean I'm effective. I mean I'm *beyond* effective. I've *arrived*! My prayers work. And yours will, too, when you begin to reign. You have received the gift of righteousness.

First of all, righteousness means right standing with God. I have right standing with Him; I have fellowship with Him; I have communion with Him; I have union with Him; and I have oneness with Him.

But it also means something else. If I have right-standing with God, then nobody else can have any better standing. Not even Jesus Christ has any better standing with God than you and I do.

Some say, "Oh, you're taking something away from Jesus!" No, He's still got the same thing He's always had; I'm just giving you something! These are things that lift us and keep our faith working.

When we know what "the gift of righteousness" means, we can stand in the presence of the devil and reign. We can rule over opposition, persecution, tests, trials, circumstances, poverty, sickness, demons, or anything else that would cause us to be a failure.

Most of the time, people have a little god about an inch and a half high. And the devil, to them, is about two and a half feet high. *The devil is not bigger than God!*

Confession:
The devil is not bigger than God.
Circumstances are not bigger than God.
Disease is not bigger than God.
My Father is greater than all.
He is my Father, and He lives in me.
He'll put me over. He'll make me a success.
I'm not afraid of anything. The Greater One is in me.
He's greater than tests and trials.
He's greater than any other power I face.
He's greater than any force that could come against me.
I expect Him, in every crisis of life, to rise up within me.
I expect Him to give illumination to my mind.
I expect Him to give strength to my body.
I expect Him to give direction unto my spirit.
He lives in me. The Greater One lives in me!
I cannot be defeated. I cannot fail.
My faith is in Him. My confidence is in Him.
I am strong in His power. Oh, glory!

Don't forget who you are. Don't forget who He is. Don't forget what He has done. Don't forget who and what He has made you!

ABOUT THE AUTHOR

The ministry of Kenneth E. Hagin has spanned more than 60 years since God miraculously healed him of a deformed heart and incurable blood disease at the age of 17. Today the scope of Kenneth Hagin Ministries is worldwide. The ministry's radio program, "Faith Seminar of the Air," is heard coast to coast in the U. S. and reaches more than 100 nations. Other outreaches include: *The Word of Faith*, a free monthly magazine; crusades, conducted nationwide; RHEMA Correspondence Bible School; RHEMA Bible Training Center; RHEMA Alumni Association and RHEMA Ministerial Association International; and a prison ministry.